STILL LIVES

Kimberly K. Williams

STILL LIVES

AND (T)HERE

What's Left Behind

Two middle-aged men by the apple tree push and pull
the branches like teenaged girls playing with hair.
They giggle, sweep back twigs, talk of baking pie.
Dull thuds mark the grass around the trunk.
When the men drive off in their golf cart,
I investigate: green balls bound into bunches

populate the space just outside my reach.
Nothing ripe remains, except one red globe
which, having escaped the primping, rolled
down the road and leaned against the curb,
its top bruised, the rest of the roundness a gathering
of sweet juice and flesh, just waiting for the bite.

Report from Manitou Springs, Colorado

Twilight at 9,000 feet: crow's tucked in, bedding
down in the branches; he's nowhere

left to fly. Night dawns quietly on the evenings
God passes through the sky. Tomorrow,

hail will pelt windows and pines and cars and crow. But so
far tonight is this: blood

orange sky drifting
into morning.

THE SWALLOWS ARE CHASING

And the swallows are chasing
God, skimming the green pools,
edging the cliffs. The swallows are
chasing God, building their nests
in the O of his name. The swallows
are chasing God, and we must chase
the swallows as far as our flat feet
and wingless backs allow: around
the fat cottonwood, over the gravel,
across the bridge that spans El Rito,
past the Bear Spotted Here notice, down
to the tip of the massive ruby sky.

Ode to the Stone Fruit

I have loved the stone
fruit. Juice and flesh grown
around inedible hardness. Summer
bounty. Skin that varies—fuzzy
or taut and smooth as a chubby
cheek. Oh baby, the tender
between the pit and the peel,
offerings in yellows, corals,
purples and reds, an end
of summer sunset. And
the words: *cherry, peach,*
plum. Nectar-ine with white
flesh. Say them slowly—
savor their ripeness on the lips.

ON THE PLAYGROUND 1

Is It
harder to say I'm sorry and mean it, or
harder to not say it if you don't
mean it?

Once upon a time,
you could erase words and leave a trace. A
dodgy remembrance & bits of rubber to
blow away.

Nowadays?
my palimpoem hustles, rustling across
the whiteness with an uneven
gait.

What Lies Beyond

The sun touches fire
to the earth's rim. The day moon's

on the rise while deep
beneath, boiling earth sears

citrine, peridot, lapis lazuli
to decorate earlobes and necks. Then

maybe dusk cradles the clouds.
Or maybe the clouds swaddle

the dusk while the slivered moon
hangs cockeyed in the sky.

Maybe. Whatever lies
beyond is nothing. We can touch.

Morning Thoughts (It Is, Part I)

It is the risk the failure the possible.
It is how will you touch me? How
I will touch you. Who will your skin

be beneath my hands? Will it come
live telling stories of wearing you
for fifty years before me? How

will it smell—of every moment gone
before you or of nothing but the rain?
What is the scent of the canteloupe

compared to the taste of its peachy
flesh behind my lips? The jasmine
stretching upward announces it's

waiting before I see it. I stop
like that. Its pulse finds mine.
Lifts it. Will it be like that?

Feeding the Seagulls, Manly, NSW

The seagulls arrive like a colony of New Yorkers, creep
forward on orange feet, razzing at a distance

before they converge. You give them only what you won't
eat: soggy tomatoes from the middle of the sandwich. As

you feed them, you think about how
you wanted a manly man. And how

you got one. He turns his head for spinning sirens and
bobbing bosoms, listens to REO Speedwagon and .38

Special. He fixes pens and broken chairs, drinks beer
from the can. You love that he knows baseball, played it,

squatting behind the plate with an open mitt, collecting
strikes & wild pitches, talking trash to the batters. His hands

that gripped the ball press your body with that loud assurance.
You are his for the taking, but only for one season.

THE GRACKLE

It is the basement bird—
naturally placed in the aviary
bargain bin. Its tail is longer

than its body, its feathers more
brown than black. It insists on hopping
(not flying) and caustic in how

it mimics a smoke detector battery
at the end of its life – one to
two screeches per skip. Yet

it's no swooping seagull. It's not even
cousin to the owl, who
with his knowing claims no

relation to what is common.
It's not the robin with its red breast.
It's not a jay bragging about blue.

It's just feathers on two legs bouncing
and grousing and blurting false
alarms beneath the tilting palm tree.

THE MAGPIE WAS ALL

We walked this
way together one
time, your hand

in my back
pocket, the jasmine brand
new & round in the air,

the light fingering brown
branches, the oaks
raising their many

hands to form a bridge,
the wind stirring
them into waves, arms

burdened by green,
& the chattering
trees silencing

the magpie was all
we needed
to say.

Maybe Some

day I'll tell you the whole—
from the way my belly tucked and flipped
at the photo of you leaning against the ute
to your choice of Singapore. (Maybe some
day. we'll arrive there.) Maybe I'll tell you—
the moment I let go and which gentle

word unleashed it. Someday I'll lower
the boom and point to the colors—sky blue
and tree green merging, the sticky shades of
grey banished to the lakes which grew me.

Maybe someday I'll remind you which song,
which lyric, where I was sitting at the National
Library when your text arrived mid-afternoon
asking me my favorite, and I'll show you
which loop I fastened myself to when
you hoisted me into your

solidity. Maybe
someday you'll see that the time you took
to explain the grill, the footy, the rockmelon
was the time it took for me to arrive at your shore,
fog lifted, sun aloft, ferry already crossing into your sea.

Cockatoo

I see your right
eye, spying me, black
peppercorn tucked

inside folds of snowy
feathers, head cocked left,
peeking over the edge

of the balcony's roof,
white shoulders against
dark slate, hopping closer

closer, curiosity
against caution
until screaming

mate behind
my head swoops down &
both birds lift & glide, wings

wide as Cessnas, curve
left—banking against
the cerulean sky.

FOLLOWING CROW

Crow suggests
the right flight
path. But no one

who's been tricked
before believes him.
Crow demonstrates

gliding in the moment before
it transforms into the next,
shows how to

notice the cottonwood
leaves shaking like coins
collected in a thief's hand.

He swoops, listening to the Arkansas'
rapids unfurl like a fist
opens into fingers.

Crow shrieks—
caws and models gratitude:
Thanks to the one

who dropped the bag of Cheetos!
But no one who's been
tricked before believes him.

at the Rise

alongside Boulder creek
where it nuzzles through the canyon
each flower bobbing in the breeze
paints her own miniature version
of the scene
hollyhock brushes
fuchsia in broad strokes and

Queen Anne’s
lace dabs ivory

and beardtongue
coats lavender in white with little
sweeps of black

each painter doing her part

to depict   the river   leaping

through the color-laden air

Say It

I would
say

  it

was a slow
      dawn,

this bonding this
l–ving slow

& steady,
  like

    rise,
the sun—

full as
      summer, takes

            its time climbing
                  the horizon.

SHE IS [NOTHING

<table>
<tr><td>but fumes and] a lick</td><td></td></tr>
<tr><td></td><td>of flame.</td></tr>
<tr><td>She dwells</td><td>in the moments</td></tr>
<tr><td></td><td>between alive & dead,</td></tr>
<tr><td>now & then. Here &</td><td>there, she comprises</td></tr>
<tr><td></td><td>condensed breath</td></tr>
<tr><td>soars in a dream,</td><td>which</td></tr>
<tr><td></td><td>dissipates when her eyelid</td></tr>
<tr><td>arches &</td><td>illuminates life.</td></tr>
</table>

Afternoon Thoughts

My eyes plunge like plums   deep within a pudding. Refractions
reveal glimpses,   but never the whole. We're all darting
minnows feeding   off small rivers. Sometimes
the bed's   dry   in high summer leaving
us stranded.   Books
crave beauty   and wilderness, but only when
open.   What do they
desire   when they're closed?
Every time   I crack
a cover   to peek, the longing in the pages
shifts again,   like syntax inverting to make a rhyme.

Never

Not a single swallow but the gulp
of them in the distance, banking
along the sunset, up cliff-
sides, brushing against
gilded fingertips
and gliding
back,

and it's not a single swallow but a swoop
of them, the whole diving towards
dusk, skimming the swimming
hole's surface and rising up
into the rafters of
night

it is never a single swallow but a richness,
cast like a net covering clouds,
then yanked towards earth,
moon crescent fastened
to pale morning
light.

THE CALL

In Tampa, when the mystery
bird's sharp caws awaken you and you listen

from bed, you understand that
he's not delivering a morning

message from the gods. He's eating
the burger left on the balcony to keep it

cold overnight. Later, when you
find the bag and its innards strewn about, the two

puncture marks in the paper
sack, you wonder

why he ate the burger but not the chicken
fingers. You

now wish you'd answered his calls,
witnessed his moment of feathered

interloping, and peeked through the hotel room curtains. But
the visit was enough—vacant,

insistent and loud, like the train that stalls at the five-point
intersection back

in Phoenix, where lines of impatient cars
form a waiting star.

June 4, Dublin

Blue sky opens
over Dublin

        at 9 p.m. like
        a harpist waiting

hands over strings
for her place

        in the song. The moon
        hangs like

a rib alongside
the plate

        of the sun. Like orange
        follows yellow,

like yellow
follows green, we

        wait until
        we decide

to return
home. We

        listen for
        the rain. Blue

sky over Dublin
and the roof-

    tops with brick
    chimneys have waited

so long,
they will stand a day

    longer, but the circling
    seagulls won't

wait a moment
more; they test

    patience & color & form, rise &
    slam into silence.

Black Bird

You are the white-
winged chough, head
dark as coal, tucked along
a branch with nine

of your brothers.
You are the one
in charge, the tired trickster
with the red-rimmed eyes.

You are the magpie, black
and white—like
us. You
don't sleep, building

and arranging your nest
without rest. You hop
when you should fly and swoop
and startle those who wander too

close. You have taught me
to wear my helmet in the spring.
Your wobbly chortle summons me, even
as you chase me away. You are a raven—all that

rowdiness hidden by branches, disappointment
audible in your "Ooh." You hail
from several continents. Part
feathers, which the wind

ruffles, part bones and beak,
you are everything
a passerine should be: restless
and proud. Running

at me with your wings aloft. Aloft, never
landing for long.

The Cleansing

Magpie taunts. The lake
down in the valley shrinks.
Bees dive for nectar.

Dragonfly leaves word,
but nothing prepared
you for today's journey, except

for the nightmare that began
the day and unsteadied
your steps as the fat and clumsy

hands batted your breasts before you
awakened. Resisting the close-mouthed
kiss incited rape, startling your

eyes open into the restless
morning. On the hillside,
you try to walk off

the dream. The sage wears purple.
The wind lassos above your head
spinning your hair into a halo.

Shedding this dream will require
an uphill haul, but sun
beams illuminate the way. Wheat

collects the light and bends it to direct
the climb. Here, now in the gusts, you
watch the grass lean. You find your

balance. You
descend on your own
accord, giving praise to the sun.

Leaving Lockdown: My Wish for You

I know I left
my hair behind
(I always do)—

strands of it
woven through-
out our brief

life. I hope
you encounter it
tucked under

a pillow when
you sleep, find
it trapped in

the carpet when
you clean, curled
against the bottom

cabinet when
you sweep. I hope
you discover my

blonde tendrils
coiled in your back-
seat or threaded

through the fly-
screen (floating
inside &

outside at one
time), drifting along-
side the pool

or tangled in
& around the potted
lemon tree leaves.

Two Days in Manly, NSW

Feb 13

The fine mist slants, soaks what it fingers
before it lands. In Manly, Norfolk pines
drop leaves long as baby
snakes. The clouds pile over
the tumbling waves—
beach empty, detritus littered

like unwashed beauty, like
brown bones bent, wary
from tumbling in the black
swells, taking several
turns several
times, disappearing before

landing on shore where
the pines offer up their branches like father
blessing the bread & the wine.
St. Mary, tucked into a brick wall nearby,
reposes in her alcove, gazing over the mountain
of movement. Meanwhile, this

instant, here at the table, the hand that foamed
the milk places the coffee. The wooden
chair scrapes the floor, dissenting.
Outside this café, eight trees
with branches arranged like ballerinas
in second position,

tutus tight & round at the hips—
gather energy & lift into fifth position,
ready to brush the impending storm.

Feb 14

The waves surge.
The piled clouds
vanish, giving way to turquoise
sky. In Manly, children & dogs
are guided & yanked past the headlands, where
they scurry around the ocean

spray, seeking
safety. It's a proper cauldron: the Pacific
sprawled beyond the metal railing, tumbling
& churning grey-brown yellow foam—crashing.
Not just movement but motion, no
smiling, just tails

tucked & the white poodle, shivering, skirts
the path's edge before the twenty-foot wave
slams the concrete wall to his right. The hushed pines
tower over the shore, swaying
where the bay bends
inward, witnessing calamity & its distance.

AT THE NATIONAL PORTRAIT GALLERY: A SEQUENCE

—(Part)

I'm unsure
what is happening even
as it occurs. It's spring, to

be sure. E.E. Cummings is on
the rise & quickens with the running
sap. (What season was he but

spring?) In this moment, I have lost my train, misplaced
my concentration, and in straying, I've discovered
something else and in finding this else I have mislaid
my sense of direction.

—All of

these accents are mine. (Little gifts the size of
syllables. Little gestures the space
of nodding.)

—And   when

his voice finds you
it arrives   like a safety

net   stretched   and waiting
not even catching you;   simply   steadiness
                                        (like

held aloft

breathing)

—(Whole)

I have wandered into
beauty: magpie chortling

by the lake, foisting
its anxiety, arguing

with itself. The sun wears
a pale yellow dress, twirls,   then stands along

the wall minding the clouds.
The security guard calls me

love, and I walk into the building
backwards. Nothing is free,

though there's no entrance fee.
        Everything around me is man-

made, except the water's ripples & the king-
parrot's whistling. When impulse lurches,

and I find myself
in an empty gallery,

what are my hands
                                        holding?

Arrival—

Beside the silent
water, the question

arrives with the cotton
tufts spinning in the wind:

What if the cottonwoods
the birds of paradise

the bougainvillea
the wet wide

blades steaming in the upper
hemisphere were pointing

down

under. Here. Where
I might settle

through
you like a breeze
bends
between

leaves. If
you'll have me.

How it Works

Most lives are lived in the corners of pages amongst numbers,

silent until read out loud, fashioned by someone else's lips until we

Sorting out paranormal from prayers requires patience. Sometimes

When we fly, we call like geese forming letters in the sky: V's and Y's

off our pages through someone else's supplication, someone else's

during the space and quiet, we startle awake, listening for echoes headers, marginalia. We are the works words make,

chatter like housecats watching wrens.

we wait for lifetimes and become the words work makes.

and W's—*do you hear me? do you?* We lift

breath, and during the lulls in formation,

that make the words work.

gathers himself in the leaves, bows 180 degrees, hind over

whistling away with a series of trills that form a single verb, a scale

When I turn, he flies closer, lands, inches across the black railing

closer and when I turn back, sensing his advancing sideways dance,

head, rises up and dips again,

of assertion.

near as anxiety allows, closer,

he darts for cover, leaving me a flower on an ornamental gate.

IN SYDNEY

I stare at the lapping underside of the world where I now live.

The green expanse behind me could be the stretch around my thoughtful placed in mid-west America, deer tiptoeing in the

to see

face noses through the blades of grass. It's raining jacaranda

This could be Mexico or even New Orleans, but it's not. Across Lavender slivers rain. Ants climb my hand. Ashes from nearby father's grave, conifers eavesdropping nearby—a bench for the distance. But it's the U of the Royal

Botanical Gardens with its string
of benches that leads to the opera house, donning Dutch
hats to deflect the sun; massive Indian figs span the path.
Kangaroos, scheduled to arrive farther along in the day,
wait on hinds,

watching the train bend round the rail, stretching up

what's on the move. The ibis with pre-history rippled across its

petals. I lean against the white wall.

the street, three adults walk, and a man pushes the pram. bushfires bump the sky.

Directions

Nothing finer than a river. Soft and quiet with skipping dragonflies.
sand and stirring silt. In the gentle eddies, gnats collect and hover
are tracks to guide it, the river will cross the world. Through the
tributary, it'll swell. Be prepared for anything. Collect pebbles and

Take off your shoes. The water is plainly cold.
the stones under your toes are sharp. Don't
stop. Understand what led you to
the water. And

when you follow
the river, meander
with the questions. If you just pay
attention, the answers might float along.

Loud and magnificent over rocks, swirling where other life breeds. As long as there desert, it will trickle. Where it meets a shiny leaves. Pick up slick stones.

Put them in your pockets.
When you lose your way, pluck
a twig from your trousers & watch which
way it floats. Go that way. In that direction.

Endeavor to avoid;
flow around the bone,
these shards of existence &
fragments of absence~

Fashioning a Romp

I walk to the hem of the suburb where it skirts the bush. There, world-class percussionists:

Plains
let,
ern
let,
ern
jo,
ble

Spot
grass
whist
tree
Pe
tree
pob
b

North
corro
frog,

mon
ern
let

despite the fog, the frogs are on their maracas, shaking them like

frog-
east-
frog-
east-
ban-
pob-
bonk.

ted
frog,
ling
frog,
ron's
frog,
le-

onk.
ern
boree
com-

east-
frog-
frog,

spot
grass
bur

frog,
and
en
and
en
frog,
frog,
ble

I come to hear them play. Magpie lands nearby, giving me the feathers. The frogs let loose their rhythms. The buzz is all. When then closer still, once more yet again, and together we two-step in

ted
and
row

green
gold-
green
gold-
bell
bell
pob-
bonk.

sideways glance. We listen together. He may be shaking his tail the cicadas join the jam session, magpie hops a half meter closer, the universal stomp.

Eye of the Tide

In the eye of the tide, everything gleams, dances, lifts, plummets, and growing, swallowing and swirling, killing the krill, takes

When the linguists arrive to examine the wreck, they find floating

ad hoc whisper rustig

ganas mentsh

wallah bitte bisous

esperar cansado

prego sláinte!

flaska hózhó

kagi köszönöm

Da. sortie nube

jak się masz

reckon balam gesund

guagua

some weighted, some floating, others churning~~syllables and cracks of the wooden slats, confusing the archaeologists who later

somersaults, so that even the baleen whale with its filter expanding
a turn.

crates, burdened with words:

farfalla

waver-

in~ ing

sha~ *lah*

obligado

stary dziadek

chuchaqui

mer-

haba

phonemes licking the salt off the water drops that lap through the
excavate the remains by gingerly brushing back sand.

AT THE NATIONAL LIBRARY, CANBERRA

Once you see your first lightning bird, you notice them every

where the grass has been recently mowed, they drop like mini-legged miner birds, creating disconcerted angels among the fat brethren to dangerous flying games.

They are stealthy. They borrow odd feathers when other birds himself when chuffed in full splendor. When they strike, lightning chicken eggs from under their roosts.

You must envy the lightning bird, who is never afraid to warble unattended in the sun. He guards against some sparkling else the mountains and thrash about for some time.

The Henry
on its side,
reposing in the

where: hanging out with the magpies on the lawn outside

bombs off the side of the building while chasing the yellow-
branches of maples alongside the lake, daring their winged

aren't looking and outright rob the peacock who cannot see beyond
birds zap instead of cry and shock instead of startle. They filch

and is always willing to shine. But do not leave your keys or coins
stealing his lightning. And then, under threat, he'll rumble towards

Moore rests
curvy figure
freshly shorn grass.

THE WORLD IS TOO MUCH

There's still wildness in the air as the world kilts out of tilter. At inside. That is the beauty of possibility. The clouds drive into town woman who brings my tart and coffee observes that it's too windy As she departs, my napkin lifts and cartwheels away.

We wear the masks because the world is too much. The dog's gone

Rumpled blanket
with striped,
purrs itself

any moment, dog becomes wolf. And every cat has feral tucked overnight and park. But they're stingy and won't gift water. The to rain. The leaves on the branch behind her rustle in agreement.

feral, and we're still trying to pet it.

overhead
grey lines
to sleep

"We suggest that the American poet E.E. Cummings was probably mildly dyslexic. Evidence, which is drawn in particular from inspection of his archival papers, includes consideration of his spelling, letter formation, handwriting, approach to page orientation, proclivity for exploration of the mirror-image, reading and educational history, struggles in the composition of analytical prose, and notable strengths in lateral thinking and the making of surprising lateral connections."

E.E. Cummings and Dyslexia
J. Alison Rosenblitt & Linda S. Siegel

On the Playground 2

Hanging up
side

down
off the monkey

bars, I stayed and light fell,
angling across
my bangs, fore-
head and eyes. Do
you believe that

a) Everything happens on
b) purpose? Everything
c) arranges itself to that
d) purpose? Some things are on
e) purpose and some things are by
f) coincidence? Nothing is
i. on purpose? How
ii. can that be when we have language that arranges itself
iii. into letters and words / patterns on paper / sounds that guide
iv. our tongues? Language, too, tracks
g) evolution. All
h) of the above.

I stayed and the light fell
asleep winding
itself into darkness
one eye

at a time. Then I departed.

sevoM ohW enO eht mA I

On, The One Who Forges Ahead;
and The One

to See
There: The

at the helm
lurch this

a) with the wind? b) in the wind?

e) it sits on
land. Nothing
remains

I Am the One Who Moves

The One Who Possibles,
Who Rushes

What's Over
great sails

of the library
ship forward:

c) because of wind? d) in spite of the wind?

unchanged (staying or
floating when [

] launches (the vast
imagination.

Still Life at Buderim Falls

I came for the
filtered light,

in the shapes of fronds.
I came to

converse with the stream, or, rather,

I came for
the whispering leaves,

rustling
The

whole, blue & black,

lay on its side,

the lightest breeze

wi

touched them together, then—

sepa

Oh, come now,

it's not

all that. There's

life

stirring

the

I didn't come
for the waterfall—

to sit
with shadows

listen to it babble.

foliage.
butterfly

wings folded,

& when put upright

caught its

ngs,

so convincingly

rated

them again.

the sun suggests,

as serious as

still

between

wings.

(T)HERE

Here Where (It Is, Part II)

The bright-blue wren animates the tiniest life here in the mountains—not the mountains I thought I'd eventually dwell in but those others, rounded and edged brown like a fireman's hands, forming the bottom

of the earth. It is those hands—not the ones I once envisioned, but the ones that arrived to grasp me—ones that extinguish wildfires, with decisive fingers that stir my embers and kindle my canopy even

as the palms douse the flaming land. It is the pine trees—not those in the Coconinos where I first believed I would end—but here where the firs filter the southern light between their needles, sheltering the paired

rosellas who depart in red streaks toward the pond. It is the lobed-shaped pond that sighs when its rim settles into the earth, its glassy eye asleep in the grass while paddling mallards nod at the brown ducks

waddling on land. The dry blades kindle / rise together / form a conflagration: flame entering / fire licking / branch transforming to ash from the moment's torch / touch transferring life / spark igniting embers

from abandoned half-lives. It is   how he holds me between those hands / in the silence / in the grass / where we lie hushed tucked inside   the yes beneath the towering gum trees.

Crows know things you don't want to consider. One crow in the hand is worth two in the ... Wait. The American in you finally understands this adage. *Bush* doesn't mean the green foliage that separated your house from the alleyway growing up.

Ravens where you reside replace the crows. You only know this because you read it. Crows don't inhabit the little region tucked inside the massive, rusted land where you now dwell. The ravens here are large as bob cats. Fat cats. Big as a tiger's head. The ravens here hop and moan. When one flies overhead, you hear its wings push the air in your direction like a lasso gaining momentum. When his beak breaks open, he speaks the same long deflated vowel: *Ohh.*

The day you realise you've been tricked is the day that the raven rises from the ashes – black as what those bush fires conjured before they extinguished. That day, your own beak cracks open and the moan barks quick, then sustains and lifts. One moment had you almost dead. But it's worse than your birdbrain could have fathomed. Now you live. And you live with this knowledge: you've been wrong all along.

Meeting Joan Miró in Manuka

At first he was a bird, flapping across the table. Then a fish. But when the waiter came, Joan ordered snapper, then asked, *How can I eat myself?* So he morphed into a rooster and then finally a man. *The cock was gratuitous* he said, cracking himself up. I said nothing, too overwhelmed by his primary presence: yellow, red, and blue splotches swarmed around his head like flies. Charcoal streaked across his cheek and nose. The waiter set down two *copas* of sangria. *Salud.* Joan tasted it and paused. *Is okay*, he said, *but I know how to make better.* He took a marker and right on the table drew a circle without moving his wrist and started coloring it in. Red Valencia, he said, as the waiter walked up with water. Looking at the orange outlined on the table, he asked me, *Who does this guy think he is? Picasso?* I shrugged, unwilling to confess the truth. When the waiter was out of earshot, Miró tapped the flat globe with his middle finger, and it popped to life. He took his butter knife and halved the fruit. Then he quartered it. Sucking on one wedge, he squeezed another into my drink then tucked the curled rind next to a cube of ice with the same finger. *Is not rioja*, he said. *But will do.*

at Malua Bay

The ocean's back to swinging her hips in rhythm rather than stretching with ungainly uncertainty at the whim of the wind. On the unfamiliar lanes, I drive around a downed tree and forget to pull left again until an oncoming car puts me in my place.

We've come at the right time—fewer people on the beach than seagulls. Blue men o'war arrived with the rising tides and made their stealthy landings. Their tentacles look like pen lines squiggled in the sand. A single pine tree overlooks the inlet. At dusk, its fingertips poke at pink and lavender, making the sky bleed just a touch.

The smallest waves whisper their proposal, and I accept. Behind me, an emergency siren wails. Each wave crashes twice into the rock I am standing on, like a door slamming a second time because the first time the latch didn't catch and what's unwanted might seep in.

Final Departure

And I'm trying to read your eyes as you try to read the departure board, but the man in the grey suit steps between us and sets his briefcase down. The flight is not delayed, it is canceled altogether. When the man retrieves his case, twenty-three years have passed, and I've not seen your eyes with my own since that day. Sometimes you send messages with your English more broken than sticks in a nest. Where I live now, ravens stand around in their glossy suits under the footbridge on campus. They look like mafioso having a quick smoke while waiting for their boss to leave the building. These black birds release sounds of sorrow, full on *Oohs* that droop at the end like disappointed children who forget that they're talking too loudly. Your latest message announces that your girlfriend has had your *oops*! baby, then mentions that I've been the best woman of your life. For a moment, I allow this to be true. The raven in the distant tree, like his campus paisanos, comprehends. Safe in his nest in the leafy green, he launches his doubtful *Oooh*.

Somewhere Between

I find you searching under the stream to see where summer's hiding as if you are looking up a lady's slip, and the crayfish startle to see your eyes peering their way. I say, *While you're at it, check for my keys*—which I lost while hiking. You don't lift your head, but you give me the thumbs up. And while I'm distracted along the bank, like a silvery minnow,

you slip away. As completely and mysteriously as my keys. Since then, I dream that others are gliding downstream. So I find myself glancing up the hems of trees or poking about under rocks, impatient for an arrival. When someone does appear with summertime in his pocket, I'll be here, somewhere between the wandering water and its shore, forgetting about my keys, forgetting about you. Ready to invite him in.

Here

The light's not right for poems, but I write anyway, feeling for the end of the spool, pinching the frayed thread, trapping it between my forefinger and thumb. I cast the spool into the blackness. It clatters on the floor. The cat, who sees all in darkness, is roused. I hear her pounce, batting the cylinder, sliding it yonder, releasing more and more line—a fishing feline. I wait until she's bored, settles down. I follow the thread, wind it, reeling in its thin life, thumbing it for possibility, tracing its nuance, chancing that I might snag an unexpected rhythm, that I might summon from the tendril a wild image. We have enough words between us all, though there are a number we forget to use. Sometimes they arrive quiet as the cat's paws, and then we all recall. At least one of us believes there will be something beautiful to make this all worthwhile. That could be you. It might be me.

What No One Expects (in Sedona)

Two javelinas round the wall like two old biddies—still spry—babushkas fastened under chins, walking close enough to whisper, stopping in tandem to acknowledge the dog at the end of my leash like they had been rehearsing this surprise encounter for days: two bristly ladies in tiny pumps clutching their handbags, adjusting their reading glasses over their snouts, squinting at the canine. *Could that be real?* they murmur, blinking in our direction, poised side-by-side, three parked cars away.

At this juncture, I'm only going to say that the moment put me in mind of bacon, and so we left the living pork to find some sizzling alongside eggs-over-easy on a plate.

EVENING THOUGHTS

With walnut acid harsh on her gums, words burn her gullet: *namely, judgment, foster, giveaway, alone*. There are new words—*anti-vaxxer, Covid, variant*—that she doesn't yet try to swallow. A few words have been so bludgeoned that they oughtn't be tasted at all: *iconic. disaster. forever.* She sees neither the forest nor the trees though dry leaves are abundant in her line of vision. She has lost track of what to look for anymore, let alone where to seek it. She picks a shell from between her teeth, glancing round. Did anybody notice the scraping? She used to worship, but people here make fun. Meaning is discarded like litter, like curled orange peels, like empty wasps nests that not even the scavengers touch. It is Covid vs. Corvid. She waits to see who triumphs.

Australian Magpie

The magpie whistles like R2D2. When he chortles, electronic musings lift from his chest and release the sounds that delighted me, at age 6, tucked inside the folding theater seat. Last week,

I came around the corner and found him at the bottom of the hill, standing mid-path, his red-rimmed eyes staring at the sun like he was watching a film. I didn't startle him. He didn't budge.

He is the mechanical trickster buried in feathers. He is flying bones lighter than my hands.

AT THE PUB IN CABBAGE TREE BAY

The bird inches out of the poem & the disc on the table moves in as the Weissbier Premium coaster with the monk knocking back a stein surprises you. A matching one resides back in Glendale, Arizona, spotting the tables in the German tavern where Fridays meant girl time & pretzels larger than your head.

The seagull with the bound leg returns hopping. The wire threads around his left limb–orange outlined in black. You've nothing for him—not even compassion because you're pretty sure he doesn't want it. He's a seagull, loud & glistening white, single webbed foot conveying him across the pavement without the need for wings.

The parcel with the serpent in the center arrives. It's from the U.S. The custom form reads: Contents: 1 Serpent. Value: $0. The gift box is ticked. Someone was thinking of you. Someone has taped over the tape over the tape. You strategize the entry – scissors or box cutter? The corner of the package has been damaged in transit, and you see a brown diamond slide against the hole and disappear again. You shake the parcel lightly. It is bottom heavy. Your very own snake! You can't wait to open it and set it down to fetch the right tool. The cat brushes against the box while purring and then walks away, her nails clicking along the hardwood floor, tail flicking behind.

(T)HERE

I see you sometimes at the edge of my vision, gaining and retracting like a pupil turning to and away from the sun. In this dimension we untied. In another dimension, we're perhaps united. And if this dimension where we're still joined is only my imagination, there couldn't be a stronger place for our union. I drive the highways with the green mountains, music, and magpies for company, and though you are not in the passenger seat, you arise in the song. In the other dimension we are romping, laughing, exploring. The back of your wide shoulders facing me, you're three steps ahead—always about to leave, always about to stay.

Checking In

You keep checking your app against the online list. Someone with Covid entered Woolworths at 11:34 on Sunday. You entered at 11:23, bought only yogurt, and left. You are in the clear. You were at the pharmacy the same time and day as a known Covid carrier, but in a different week. It is dodgeball. That game you hated as a child, the hyper over-zealous boys hurling their fears in the shape of loud, red balls. When they smacked against you, turning your pale skin pink, you were penalized and called out. Forty years later, scrolling through the list, you absently rub your elbow against the early lessons that never fully fade.

Self-Portrait

The woman who no one speaks to chats to herself. And sings to her cat with the pink nose. They both chatter at the magpies. She's become *that woman*, talking to herself in public and appearing a bit untidy, wearing her pink sunhat askew with the white plastic headphones on top. This ensures that she chats louder than the magpies' chortle. She breaks walnut meats in her palm and scatters them mixed with pistachios and pepitas. Each day the juveniles creep closer and sometimes run to greet her, puffed chests and stretched wings the color of an angry sky.

Touched

At one time or another, we're each touched by gods. Even if it's just in passing, like the time I was climbing this marble staircase, and Aphrodite came tumbling down, and the bottom of her sandal brushed my calf as she whished by with Adonis in pursuit.

Other times, the gods are buried, like the stone in a plum, and our human touch releases them, as teeth break through skin, cutting red flesh before finding its pit, and I tongue the roughness, wondering if gods ever enter through my parted lips.

No Body

I set off in my body and, along the trek,
encounter so many other selves I can't
recall them all. The smell of cinnamon
invites one; the scent of jasmine another.
The taste of black coffee collects the self
who settles cross-legged on the sofa to sip.
I am gentler with my selves now as if I've
become the slip

beneath the dress instead of the outfit
itself. When I am tired, we all nap, and
one of them rouses the rest of us from our
prone positions as we awaken. At some
point our body will lie down and release
a few of us while the uncountable rest
cartwheel through the dusk.

Just When

you least expect it / it becomes normal to carry a sharpened stick / to count time with each footfall. We used / to tiptoe, but there's a softness / somewhere that's hardened./ Fossilized. We tuck in the crevices, and thirty million years onward when someone dredges us out or cracks / us open, we'll be here. And there. Nothing's changed. I've reached a space and expanded to fill it / but I'm too busy. Hiding.

Lost in Space

Daily, I scrawl notes, writing pages of phrases wherein I can't say what I think. Not saying takes more words than saying, and so I compose those spaces, too. Because I write what I don't think, I don't remember what I write: *Please provide the word count. Please don't use the font that* floats. *Please give your story a title.* What they write is single-spaced and travels across the page like pilgrims walking down a road. *Please tether your letters to the page.* Because I write what I don't think, I don't remember what I write, though I produce many pages of it. Then when I do want to remember what I wrote, I don't. *I'm sorry, as I already mentioned, this font* **floats** *when I read it.*

Consider the Spider

who on eight legs waits for the fly. He's no need of the magpie hustling in the distance. He's no need of the humans lurching beneath his post. He's no need of the climbing wisteria that's inviting the bee to dine. He only requires the instinct of the fly and the sticky curiosity that delivers him home.

Colors for Kiev

By coincidence (which is never pure) everyone wears the white vestments of angels & bears a candle. A beige paper circle wraps the lower end of each ivory stick, catching what drips. A monk in a brown robe nods a each person's exit. As we follow the path from the catacombs, the flames we carry waver, flicker, and fade into the day. The air smells of wax, extinguished fire, and coffee from the nearby cafe, where one woman's cup sloshes dark splotches across her tunic. Outside, above is as blue as a turquoise ring & golden domes gild the sky.

Here &

(for JC)

My dreams insist on loving you. Not sentimental love. No floating hearts or croon-y tunes—just us two, kneeling side by side, palms guiding flames, together offering what can't be named. Just you and me cupping the licks of light gingerly, as one might return a ladybug to her leaf.

There

Another dream shows you at age six, standing between your parents, balancing on the front seat while your father drives; in another, you stand long and tall between two pillars, leaning against one, hands tucked in pockets, feet crossed at the ankles—all your beauty fierce. All that ferocity distant. All that distance commanding this love.

Even One

I refuse to sing today, refuse to turn the universal key and let myself in, because I am FSFM — feeling sorry for myself. As if commiserating, the magpies have made themselves disappear. I don't see even one on my path uphill where they usually stand around in their fitted tuxedos.

I refuse to sing today, and I won't acknowledge the moon's paltry crescent. Exhausted by the earth's gravity and dizzied by her incessant spinning, I palm my eyes. If I can't see her, she won't see me.

My recalcitrance grows

opulent, like the sheen of a raven. And I refuse to sing in any way today. No lyrics. No notes. Just the knocking of the washing machine off kilter and my head filled like a jar of angry bees. I tighten the lid, place the glass to my ear and shake it. Generate more buzz.

Deep Like the River
(after Langston Hughes)

I am obsessed with rivers.

I wander the banks, sizing up the river: snake-like in its windings, Zen-like in its pools, frightened when rushing at the lip of the waterfall, exuberant and laughing when it lands among itself without calamity, then zips along.

While others
stroll beaches and ponder the surf, the tides, the horizon, I walk the edges, skirt the reeds, listen to the liquid babble, the songbirds twitter, the ducks squabble—language risen as a host before the mouth is ever reached.

I finger the pebbles
that line the river's route, fill the cup of my hand with its coolness as a red tulip cradles sun. I am obsessed with the river; its ancient trickles, its rages, its roars and whirling loops, dark waters jetting forwards, dusky waters spinning out our dreams.

You are obsessed with rivers.

You take your body down to the river. You remove your sandals. You sink your feet into the chill, letting your toes hug the pebbles beneath. You wade, every step pulling you deeper into the current, the water level line creeping up your thighs.

When it embraces your hips, you lift your legs like a frog and breaststroke toward the rapid. You launch yourself into the glory, with the cottonwood leaves overhead dappling light across the river's skin, across your body that shimmies along.

You dip as the white cap slingshots your body, jetties you towards a boulder, then swings you into an eddy where you float like a circling stick.

You took your body down to the river. The river took your body and taught it to swim.

Now you and the river go everywhere together.

THE STILLNESS BETWEEN

The noisy miner birds step off the ledge of the building like kids pogo-sticking into the deep end of a pool. Brown bundles drop past my window, moving in single file. The littlest one cries at the edge of the roof. Now he is far behind the others. We wait, both of us uncertain, studying the air between us.

I follow the path through the weeds like a stream follows its route – collecting, sloughing, and seething where the rocks are jagged. One shoe following the next startles the dirt into dust. And I wonder, though we often prize the plunge, if it's staying the course that counts.

Still Lives
by Kimberly K. Williams

for my sisters, Laura Sensing and Allyson Williams-Yee

Acknowledgement is made to the following publications in which these poems first appeared: 'The Grackle' and 'The Swallows Are Chasing' *Silence: The University of Canberra Vice Chancellor's International Poetry Prize* International Poetry Studies Institute, 2019; 'At the Rise' and 'Never', *The Blue Nib*, 2020; 'Leaving Lockdown: My Wish for You' *The Incompleteness Book II: Writing Back and Thinking Forward*, Australasian Association of Writing Programs and Recent Work Press, 2021; 'At the National Portrait Gallery,' *Cordite Poetry Review*, November 2021; 'Maybe the Moon' *This Gift This Poem*, Puncher & Wattmann, 2021.

First published 2022

POETRY

ISBN: 978-0-6454648-6-3

BOOK, TYPSETTING, AND LOGO DESIGN
Mountains Brown Press

PUBLISHER
Life Before Man

Gazebo Books
PO Box 375
Summer Hill
New South Wales 2130
Australia

gazebobooks.com.au/life-before-man/

2 4 6 8 10 9 7 5 3 1

COVER IMAGE: *Beam*, 2022, oil on copper, 45 x 30 cm, © Phil Day

ISBN 978-0-6454648-6-3

www.ingramcontent.com/pod-product-compliance
Lightning Source LLC
LaVergne TN
LVHW051005080826
845145LV00009B/2461

9780645464863